THE JESUS I NEVER KNEW

Participant's Guide

Books by Philip Yancey

The Jesus I Never Knew
What's So Amazing About Grace?
Where Is God When It Hurts?
Disappointment with God
The Student Bible, NIV (with Tim Stafford)
Church: Why Bother?
Discovering God
Finding God in Unexpected Places
The Jesus I Never Knew Study Guide (with Brenda Quinn)
What's So Amazing About Grace? Study Guide
   (with Brenda Quinn)

Books by Dr. Paul Brand and Philip Yancey

Fearfully and Wonderfully Made
In His Image
The Gift of Pain

THE
JESUS I
NEVER
KNEW

Participant's Guide

PHILIP YANCEY
written by Sheryl Moon

ZondervanPublishingHouse
Grand Rapids, Michigan

A Division of HarperCollins*Publishers*

The Jesus I Never Knew Participant's Guide
Copyright © 1998 by Philip D. Yancey

Requests for information should be addressed to:

📖 ZondervanPublishingHouse
Grand Rapids, Michigan 49530

ISBN: 0–310–22433–0

Interior design by Sue Vandenberg Koppenol

Printed in the United States of America

98 99 00 01 02 03 04 /❖ ML/ 10 9 8 7 6 5

Contents

Introduction

Philip Yancey's study of Jesus began with a class he taught at LaSalle Street Church in Chicago. The use of movies about the life of Jesus, the discussion from class members, and his personal study all combined to give him a new view of Jesus—hence the title of his book *The Jesus I Never Knew.*

Yet all along he had another goal in mind: He wanted his quest for Jesus to serve as a guide for other people. As Yancey himself wrote, "In the end, what does it matter if a reader learns about 'The Jesus Philip Yancey Never Knew?' What matters infinitely more is for *you* to get to know Jesus."

You are about to engage yourself in a 14-session study that is bound to change your perceptions of who Jesus is. In each session you will see several film depictions of Jesus, his life and his ministry. Some will be funny, some will be profound, and some will even be disturbing. After reacting to the film clips you will turn to the Gospel accounts of these same scenes and discuss what you believe really happened. Obviously the filmmakers used their own interpretations of what happened. The film clips are there to help us think about Jesus in a new way—to examine our own preconceived ideas in comparison with what the Bible teaches.

For those who have been raised in the church and have known Jesus all of their lives, *and* for those who are meeting Jesus for the first time, Philip Yancey challenges us to think about this man as the Bible presents him—brilliant, creative, challenging, fearless, compassionate, unpredictable, and ultimately satisfying. You will find that the video clips combined with the Bible study and your own discussion will help you to discover the Jesus *you* never knew!

Session One:
The Jesus
I Thought I Knew

Questions To Consider

- How do I perceive Jesus?

- Who is Philip Yancey, and how can films help me to see Jesus in a new way?

- What is *my* answer to the question, "Who is this man, Jesus?"

The Twentieth-Century View of Jesus

What one word would a church member choose to describe Jesus?

How would one of your neighbors or one of your coworkers describe Jesus?

In your mind's eye, what did Jesus look like? Tall? Short? Handsome? Curly hair or straight? Did he have a dark or light complexion? Where did you get this picture of him (films, paintings, books, Sunday school)? Can you describe specific images from the past?

Video Notes
Philip Yancey

As you watch the following scenes from these three films, think of one adjective or impression that describes your reactions or feelings. If you need some help, use the questions below as a guide.

Kings of Kings

Is this like the image of Jesus you had growing up?

The Gospel According to St. Matthew

Do you find anything disturbing about Pasolini's Jesus?

Son of Man

Can you imagine Jesus being overweight?
Can you imagine Jesus ever saying, "Shut up!"?

Personal Reflection

In the first column the various stages of your life are listed for you. For each stage think of the major people and events that influenced you. Record your responses in column 2. In column 3 jot down how you related to or experienced Christ at that time.

Stage of Life	Major Influence	My Experience/ Thoughts/Relationship
Childhood		
Teen Years		
College Days		
Adult Life		

Facts About Jesus

- The birth of Jesus _____ history.

- _____-_____ of all people on earth claim to be Christians.

- The name of Jesus has become _____,
  even used as a _____ _____.

The perceptions we have of Jesus have been muddied by:

- _____

- _____

- _____

And yet, the question remains, "_____ _____ _____
_____?"

Bible Study

1. Read Mark 6:1–6. What does this passage tell us about Jesus?

2. Do you think people today have any clearer picture of who Jesus is than did the people in his day? How do you think Jesus feels about the confusing portrait presented in today's church or by some individuals?

3. What impact do you think this type of study may have on your perceptions of who Jesus is? What do you hope might happen in this study as you take a new look at Jesus?

4. What scares you most about getting to know the real Jesus?

Summary

In this session we:

- Looked at the various ways people perceive Jesus.

- Were introduced to Philip Yancey and the film approach used throughout this course.

- Learned that the bottom line is for each of us to answer the question, "Who is this man, Jesus?"

Suggested Reading

For more thoughts on this session's topic, read
"The Jesus I Thought I Knew," chapter 1
of *The Jesus I Never Knew*.

Session Two:
Birth:
The Visited Planet

Questions To Consider

- In what ways do our Christmas cards clarify or confuse our understanding of Christ's coming?

- What do the circumstances surrounding Jesus' birth teach us about God?

A Christmas-Card Christmas

What kinds of scenes are often presented on our Christmas cards?

What types of sentiments do our Christmas cards convey?

What kind of message about Jesus do these Christmas cards send to those who are not Christians?

Video Notes

Heaven

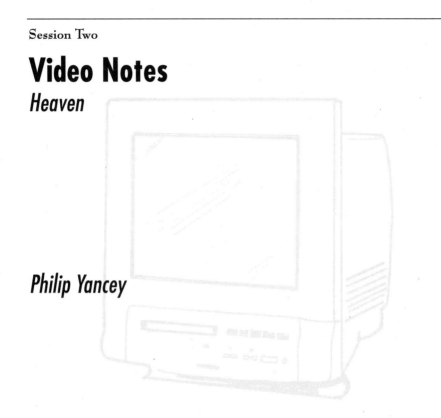

Philip Yancey

Jesus of Nazareth

Small Group Discussion

1. What struck you as you watched the films? If Diane Keaton had asked *you*, "What is God like?" what would you have said?

2. Can you see why people might have difficulty understanding how the God of the universe could come to earth as a *baby*?

3. Put yourself in the place of Mary or Joseph. How would you have responded to the angel's announcements?

4. How do you think you would have responded to Mary and Joseph's situation if you had been a member of their extended family? Critically? Skeptically? Supportively? With understanding?

Bible Study

Read: Matthew 1:18–25 (virgin conception)
        Luke 2:1–20 (shepherds)
        Matthew 2:1–12 (wise men)

1. How does the biblical account compare/contrast with what we saw depicted in the films? In the Christmas cards?

2. Which aspect of the story seems most incredible to you? Why?

3. What new idea have you had today concerning Jesus' birth?

4. If Jesus were born in the 1990s, what set of circumstances would parallel those of 2000 years ago?

5. In what ways do you think Jesus was a typical child? In what ways was he different?

6. What do we learn about God from the birth of Jesus?

Summary

In this session we:

- Explored some of the ways our Christmas cards clarify and confuse our understanding of Christ's coming.

- Identified what the circumstances surrounding Jesus' birth teach us.

Suggested Reading

For more thoughts on this session's topic, read
"Birth: The Visited Planet," chapter 2
of *The Jesus I Never Knew*.

Session Three:
Background: Jewish Roots and Soil

Questions To Consider

- How much do I know about Jewish culture (and therefore Jesus' Jewishness)?

- When Jesus was on earth, what was the religious/political climate in Palestine?

- How would I have responded to the religious pressure in Jesus' day?

Jewish Culture

Do you know someone who is Jewish? Describe that individual. What do you appreciate about his or her Jewish heritage?

What are some of the stereotypes or misconceptions about Jews?

If you are Jewish, what has been your experience with people who are not Jewish? Have you ever felt prejudice from non-Jewish Christians? Even if you are not Jewish, have you ever been in a position in which you have felt like a member of a minority?

Share with the class your knowledge of one Jewish custom or holiday.

Video Notes
Philip Yancey

Gospel Road

Cotton Patch Gospel

Religious Leaders Within the Jewish Community

Eight million Jews lived in the Roman empire in Jesus' day, just over a quarter of them in Palestine itself. In many ways, the plight of the Jewish leaders resembled that of the Russian churches under Stalin. They could cooperate, which meant submitting to government interference, or they could go their own way, which meant harsh persecution. In response, Jews splintered into five parties that followed different paths of collaboration or separatism.

1. E_____ (Matthew 6:1–4)

2. Z_____ (Matthew 5:43–48)

3. S_____ (Matthew 7:1–6)

4. S_____ (Matthew 5:17–20)

5. P_____ (Matthew 5:21–26)

Small Group Discussion

1. As Christians today respond to an increasingly secular society, do they adopt approaches similar to those of these groups? Can you think of leaders or groups today who resemble these groups of Jesus' day?

2. Which group do you think you would have associated yourself with during Jesus' lifetime? Which of the five groups do you have a tendency to resemble within the context of our culture? Would Jesus have won you over?

3. Why is it so difficult to align ourselves with Jesus' message and ministry?

Summary

In this session we:

- Clarified our views and perceptions of Jewish culture.

- Identified the religious/political climate in Palestine during Jesus' life and learned about the five different groups of religious leaders at that time.

- Reflected upon our own response to the religious pressures in Jesus' day and in our own lives.

Suggested Reading

For more thoughts on this session's topic, read
"Background: Jewish Roots and Soil,"
chapter 3 of *The Jesus I Never Knew*.

Session Four:
Temptation: Showdown in the Desert

Questions To Consider

- How do we experience temptation in our world?

- What was the true nature of Jesus' temptation in the desert?

- In what ways do we face the same temptations Jesus did?

What *Is* Temptation?

How would you define "temptation"?

What are some of the temptations you face on a daily basis?

Get out of school
and go back to steel

At your job

to leave the kares

With the media—TV, movies, music, the Internet

To turn tv off

With your family

to get rid of bind

In your leisure time

If I am sick
I want to go Outside

How does our society view temptation?

to go home?

Video Notes

Heaven

Philip Yancey

Cotton Patch Gospel

Bible Study

Read Matthew 4:1–11—"Satan Tempts Jesus in the Desert"

Satan's temptation focused on three crucial areas: (1) economics, (2) spiritual power, and (3) political power. As Malcolm Muggeridge sees it (see the exact quote in Yancey's book, pp. 72–73), the Temptation concerned the question uppermost in the minds of Jesus' countrymen: What should the Messiah look like?
A *people's* Messiah, who could turn stones into bread to feed the multitudes?
A *Torah* Messiah, standing tall at the lofty pinnacle of the temple?
A *king* Messiah, ruling over not just Israel but all the kingdoms of earth?

1. What kind of Messiah are you looking for? Do you want a God who will fix social problems and relieve the suffering in our world? Or a God who unites all the churches and clarifies the one right way? Or a God who brings worldwide peace? Or maybe you're more drawn to a God who will meet all your needs? Or a God who will guarantee your health and safety? Or a God who will cause others to respect and acclaim you? Is there anything wrong in having these hopes or expectations of God?

2. What do Jesus' responses to Satan tell us about how we are to respond to temptation?

Small Group Discussion

In his book, Philip Yancey writes:

> I want God to take a more active role in my personal history. I want quick and spectacular answers to my prayers, healing for my diseases, and protection and safety for my loved ones. I want a God without ambiguity, one to whom I can point for the sake of my doubting friends.
>
> When I think these thoughts, I recognize in myself a thin, hollow echo of the challenge that Satan hurled at Jesus two thousand years ago. God resists those temptations now as Jesus resisted them on earth, settling instead for a slower, gentler way.

Do you ever wish Jesus would "hurry up" his work in your life—for example, in your job, dating relationships, friendships, marriage, raising your children, volunteer work, success in your church? What makes you spiritually impatient? What do you do with that impatience? Are you tempted to compromise Jesus' way to achieve what you want?

Summary

In this session we:

- Identified some of the day-to-day things that tempt us.

- Discovered the true nature of Jesus' temptation in the desert: taking a "shortcut" to what was rightfully his.

- Evaluated our lives in light of what tempted Jesus: (1) physical needs and desires, (2) possessions and power, and (3) pride.

Suggested Reading

For more thoughts on this session's topic, read
"Temptation: Showdown in the Desert,"
chapter 4 of *The Jesus I Never Knew.*

Session Five:
Profile: What Would I Have Noticed?

Questions To Consider

- What impressions do you have of Jesus' physical attributes, personality, and ministry?

- What characteristics of Jesus stand out?

  melo   he was not pushy

- What does the Bible tell us about Jesus' message and ministry?

Characteristics of Jesus

What words would you use to characterize Jesus as you already know him?

His physical attributes

Strong power full and peace full

His personality

made

Sometimes

 His ministry *He did not tell them what to do*

When in your life did you form these impressions? What/who influenced you? *I get confused*

do

Video Notes
Philip Yancey

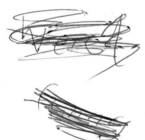

reporter

obzvers

Witnesses

he is crazy

Bible Study

As you read the following Scripture passages, give just a word or phrase to describe the emotions or personality characteristics Jesus displays.

Matthew 27:46

Mark 1:40–41

Mark 3:1–5

Mark 6:30–31

Mark 6:34   *pity   commpation*

Mark 14:34–36

Luke 10:21

Luke 19:41–44

Luke 23:34

Luke 23:43

Luke 23:46

Bible Study (continued)

Read Luke 10:25–37—The Parable of The Good Samaritan. Try to
imagine that you are hearing this story for the first time.

1. How would you have felt at the end of this story if you were:

The expert in the law who asked Jesus the question, "Who is my
neighbor?"

guilty   *good*

A priest, Levite, or a Samaritan,

One of Jesus' disciples, *help him they would have understood*

An onlooker in the crowd?

2. How do you typically respond to those around you who are in need:
   physically, spiritually, emotionally? *I don't know*

3. As our study progresses and Jesus continues to reveal himself, are
   you attracted to him? His personality? His message? Would you find
   him threatening? *don't know*

Summary

In this session we:

- Reflected upon our impressions of Jesus' physical attributes, personality, and ministry.

- Learned about Jesus' outstanding characteristics.

- Explored what the Bible has to teach us about Jesus' message and ministry.

Suggested Reading

For more thoughts on this session's topic, read:
"Profile: What Would I Have Noticed?";
chapter 5 of *The Jesus I Never Knew*.

Session Six:
Beatitudes: Lucky Are the Unlucky

Questions To Consider

- In the past, what has been your response to the Beatitudes?

- Why is the message of Jesus so difficult for us to grasp?

- What new insights can we gain if we look at the Beatitudes in a new way?

Beati-what?

What feelings/experiences have you had as you studied the Beatitudes in the past? The hope that god is alwas with us!

Have you ever considered following the Beatitudes literally?

Why do you think it is difficult for us to take the Beatitudes seriously? Do Christians try to follow some of the Beatitudes and let the rest go? Are these words of Jesus just nice phrases that sound good but have no practical relevance? When is the last time you seriously considered this passage of Scripture?

The Teaching of Jesus

Philip Yancey says: Though I have tried at times to dismiss the Sermon
on the Mount as _____ _____, the more I study Jesus,
the more I realize that the statements contained here lie at the
_____ of his _____ . If I fail to _____ this teaching, I fail to understand _____ .

The Beatitudes _____ to us on at least three levels:

1. Dangled Promises—The Beatitudes give us the _____
   _____ _____. They are a _____ ___ _____. They
   allow us to believe in a just God after all.

2. The Great Reversal—The Beatitudes describe the _____ as
   well as the _____. They express that God views the world
   through a _____ set of _____.

3. Psychological Reality—The Beatitudes reveal that what brings us
   success in the _____ ___ _____ also benefits us
   most in _____ _____.

Video Notes
Jesus

Philip Yancey

Small Group Discussion

J. B. Phillips rendered this version of the Beatitudes as they apply in the kingdom of this world:

Happy are the "pushers": for they get on in the world.
Happy are the hard-boiled: for they never let life hurt them.
Happy are they who complain: for they get their own way in the end.
Happy are the blasé: for they never worry over their sins.
Happy are the slave-drivers: for they get results.
Happy are the knowledgeable men of the world: for they know their way around.
Happy are the trouble-makers: for they make people take notice of them.

1. What is your initial reaction to this paraphrase?

2. These words seem to reflect the values of our culture. What meaning can the Beatitudes have for a society that honors the self-assertive, the confident, and the rich?

Personalized Beatitudes

How do these statements reflect your values and behaviors? Choose one or two that you especially need to think and pray about.

- I am blessed because in my loneliness, my fears, and my inner struggles, God has promised me a beautiful future. That promise helps me see my struggles with new eyes.

- I am blessed as I grieve. In the depths of my sorrow Jesus meets me and mourns with me, bringing comfort in unexpected ways.

- I am blessed in choosing not to exalt myself. This means I get overlooked at times, but I'm living for God, not for the acclaim of men and women. Someday I'll be glad I chose the way of humility.

- I am blessed in my yearning to live as Jesus did. God is faithful to me as I ponder Jesus' righteous ways and pray for the Spirit to guide how I live and who I am.

- I am blessed because I choose to show mercy, even when others don't really deserve it. I see much in me that is undeserving, yet Jesus has been merciful again and again.

- I am blessed because I'm careful about what I do, see, read, and think about. I want to be pure because this is when I can see God most clearly. This is when I am closest to God.

- I am blessed because I long for peace among those around me. I desire to enter into the world of others to better understand and come alongside them. I'm willing to do what is uncomfortable for the sake of peace, following in the footsteps of Jesus.

- I am blessed when, because of my loyalty to Jesus, others look down on me, violate my God-given rights, lie about me with evil intent, or hurt me. This world is not my home, and persecution blesses me because it is a reminder of the kingdom of heaven that awaits me not so far away. For "no eye has seen, no ear has heard, no mind has conceived what God has prepared for those who love him" (1 Cor. 2:9).

Summary

In this session we:

• Reflected upon our past interpretations of the Beatitudes.

• Explored the teaching of Jesus.

• Discovered new insights into the Beatitudes.

Suggested Reading

For more thoughts on this session's topic, read
"Beatitudes: Lucky Are the Unlucky,"
chapter 6 of *The Jesus I Never Knew*.

Session Seven:
Message: A Sermon of Offense

Questions To Consider

- What kinds of things offend people?

- Does the Sermon on the Mount have anything to say to us today?

- How do we maintain high ideals while offering a safety net of grace?

Offended? Who, Me?

If you are familiar with the Sermon on the Mount, have you ever considered its message "offensive"?

In our culture, what messages from the church do people often find offensive?

In the church, what kinds of things offend people? What kinds of things offend *you* (honestly!)?

Scripture Reading:
The Sermon on the Mount

Matthew 5:13–16	Salt and Light
Matthew 5:17–20	The Law
Matthew 5:21–26	Anger
Matthew 5:27–30	Lust
Matthew 5:32–32	Divorce
Matthew 5:33–36	Vows
Matthew 5:37–42	Retaliation
Matthew 5:43–47	Loving Enemies
Matthew 6:1–4	Giving to the Needy
Matthew 6:5–15	Prayer
Matthew 6:16–18	Fasting
Matthew 6:19–24	Money
Matthew 6: 25–34	Worry
Matthew 7:1–6	Criticizing Others
Matthew 7:7–12	Asking, Seeking, Knocking
Matthew 7:13–14	Way to Heaven
Matthew 7:15–20	Fruit in People's Lives
Matthew 7:21–28	People Who Build Houses on Rock and Sand

Bible Study Questions

Read two or three of the passages found on the preceding page and answer the following questions as they pertain to each passage.

1. What principle does this passage present?

2. Why do you think this message was offensive to those who heard it? Why might it be offensive to those who read it today?

3. What does this passage teach us about God?

4. How does this passage apply in today's settings?

Personal Application

1. It's much easier to study God's laws and tell others to obey them than to put them into practice. How are *you* doing at obeying God?

2. When do you keep God's *rules* but close your eyes to his *intent?*

Video Notes
Philip Yancey

The Gospel According to St. Matthew

Son of Man

Summary

In this session we:

- Identified areas where people often are offended.

- Studied the Sermon on the Mount to discover what it has to say to us today.

- Reflected upon the difficulty of maintaining high ideals while still offering a safety net of grace.

Suggested Reading

For more thoughts on this session's topic, read
"Message: A Sermon of Offense,"
chapter 7 of *The Jesus I Never Knew*.

Session Eight:
Mission:
A Revolution
of Grace

Questions To Consider

- Who are the "outcasts" of society?

- How did Jesus communicate God's grace?

- How does/can *our* church communicate mercy toward sinners *and* encourage genuine worship of Jesus?

"Outcasts"

Can you think of individuals or groups who are considered "outcasts" in the Bible?

Which individuals or groups are sometimes considered "outcasts" in our world today?

Video Notes
Philip Yancey

Gospel Road

Jesus of Nazareth

Bible Study

Read Matthew 9:9–13—"Jesus Eats with Sinners at a Tax Collector's House"

In Jesus' day tax collectors collected taxes on a commission basis, pocketing whatever profits they could extort from the locals. Most Jews viewed them as traitors serving the Roman empire. The words tax collector were synonymous with robber, brigand, murderer, and reprobate. Jewish courts considered a tax collector's evidence as invalid, and his money could not be accepted as alms for the poor or used in exchange since it had been acquired by such despicable means.

It seems that the more unsavory the characters, the more at ease they seemed to feel around Jesus. In contrast, Jesus got a chilly response from more respectable types. How strange that now the Christian church attracts respectable types who closely resemble the people most suspicious of Jesus on earth. What has happened to reverse the pattern of Jesus' day? Why don't sinners like being around Christians and the church today?

On a scale of 1 to 10, how is our church doing in attracting sinners to our fellowship?

Let's consider that topic in greater detail. Go to the next page and discuss the questions there. Choose one person from your group to highlight one or two points of your discussion to be shared with the entire class.

Small Group Discussion

1. How does/can our church communicate mercy toward sinners?

   Preaching

   Worship service format

   Programs

   Community service

2. How does/can our church encourage genuine worship of Jesus?

   Preaching

   Worship service format

   Lay people participating in worship

   Music

   Sunday school

   Small groups

   Other programs

3. What can we/I do to help our church in this process?

Summary

In this session we:

- Identified the "outcasts" in the Bible and in our society.

- Studied the way in which Jesus communicated grace.

- Identified ways in which our church does and can communicate mercy toward sinners *and* encourage genuine worship of Jesus.

Suggested Reading

For more thoughts on this session's topic, read
"Mission: A Revolution of Grace,"
chapter 8 of *The Jesus I Never Knew*.

Session Nine:
Miracles: Snapshots of the Supernatural

Questions To Consider

- What was your view of miracles as you were growing up?

- What were some of the miracles of Jesus, and why did he do them?

- What lessons from the miracles of Jesus can we apply today?

Miracles

What was your view of miracles as you were growing up?

List some of the miracles of Jesus that you recall.

Take a look at two or three of your responses. Why did Jesus do them? What was his motivation?

Video Notes

Jesus

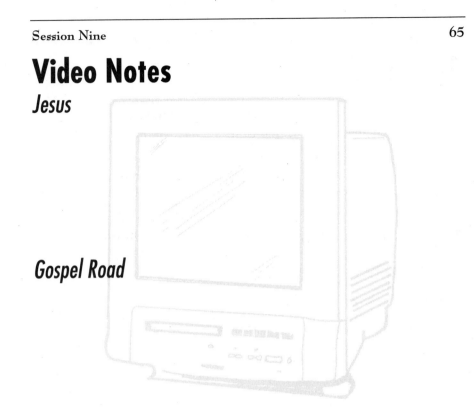

Gospel Road

Philip Yancey

Bible Study

Read one of the following passages describing a miracle that Jesus performed and then answer the questions, choosing one key idea to share with the whole group.

John 2:1–11   Wine at the wedding feast of Cana
Matthew 14:15–21   Feeding of the 5,000
Matthew 9:20–22   Healing of the bleeding woman
Mark 9:14–29   Healing of the boy with an evil spirit
Matthew 8:28–34   Demons sent into the pigs
Luke 17:11–19   Healing of the ten with leprosy

1. What does this passage tell you about Jesus?

2. What kind of impact did this miracle have on those around the situation at the time: family, friends, the crowd, the religious leaders? Is there any indication that people acknowledged Jesus as the Messiah because of this miracle? Or is there any indication that people's faith was increased?

3. Why do you think Jesus chose to perform this particular miracle?

4. Does Jesus still work miracles of this sort in similar situations? What is usually the outcome if this type of miracle does occur? What *might* be the outcome if it did?

5. What have you learned in this session that has been new for you?

Summary

In this session we:

- Discussed our various impressions of miracles when we were children.

- Identified some of the miracles of Jesus and tried to ascertain his motivation for doing them.

- Applied some of the lessons Jesus taught through his miracles to our own lives.

Suggested Reading

For more thoughts on this session's topic, read
"Miracles: Snapshots of the Supernatural,"
chapter 9 of *The Jesus I Never Knew*.

Session Ten:
Death:
The Final Week

Questions To Consider

- In what ways do we commemorate Holy Week, the week *before* Easter?

- Why is the death of Jesus such a critical event?

- What do we learn about Jesus in each of the events leading up to and including his death: the Triumphal Entry, the Last Supper, his trial, and his crucifixion?

- What is my *personal* response to the death of Jesus Christ?

Celebrating Holy Week

How does our church celebrate Holy Week, the week before Easter?

What other activities have you experienced to commemorate Holy Week?

Video Notes
Philip Yancey

Witnesses

Bible Study
The Triumphal Entry

Read Luke 19: 28–44

1. What is happening in this passage?

2. Why is this event significant?

3. Is this event the same or different from some of Jesus' other interactions with the crowds at different times in his ministry? Explain.

4. How would you have responded to this event had you been in the crowd that day? If you were one of Jesus' disciples? If you were one of the religious rulers?

Bible Study
The Last Supper

Read Matthew 26:26–29

1. What is happening in this passage?

2. Why is this event significant?

3. Is this event the same or different from some of Jesus' other interactions with his disciples at different times in his ministry? Explain.

4. How would you have felt if you had been one of the disciples that day?

Bible Study
Jesus on Trial

Matthew 26:57–27:2, 11–31

1. What is happening in this passage?

2. Why is this event significant?

3. As Jesus' stands before the authorities, is his behavior the same or different from other times in his ministry? Explain.

4. How would you have responded to this event had you been in the crowd that day? If you were one of Jesus' disciples? If you were one of the religious rulers?

Bible Study
The Crucifixion

Read Matthew 27:31–56

1. What is happening in this passage?

2. Why is this event significant?

3. How would you have felt if you had been in the crowd that day? If you were one of Jesus' disciples? If you were one of the religious rulers? If you were visiting the city just for the day?

4. What does the Crucifixion teach us about God?

Personal Reflection

1. Having been through this session, how has my understanding grown regarding Jesus' final week on earth?

2. What can/will I do during the next Lenten period to observe Holy Week in a meaningful way?

3. Do I truly believe that Jesus died for *me*? How is this belief reflected in my everyday life?

Summary

In this session we:

* Reflected on the various ways we commemorate Holy Week.

* Identified why the death of Jesus is such a critical event.

* Discovered some important truths regarding the events leading up to and including Jesus' death: the Triumphal Entry, the Last Supper, his trial, and the Crucifixion.

* Considered our response to the death of Christ.

Suggested Reading

For more thoughts on this session's topic, read
"Death: The Final Week,"
chapter 10 of *The Jesus I Never Knew*.

Session Eleven:
Resurrection: A Morning Beyond Belief

Questions To Consider

- How do we celebrate Easter today?

- What *really* happened on the first Easter?

- How do we deal with the doubts we may have about Jesus' resurrection?

Easter!

What Easter experiences have you had that have been truly
meaningful?

What Easter experiences have you had that have been negative?

Video Notes
Philip Yancey

King of Kings

Cotton Patch Gospel

Small Group Discussion

1. The first Christians staked everything on the Resurrection, so much so that the apostle Paul told the Corinthians, "And if Christ has not been raised, our preaching is useless and so is your faith." Did it *really* happen—this event, apart from which our faith is useless? How can we be sure?

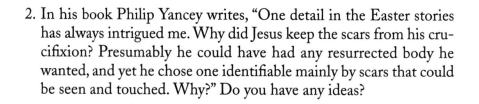

2. In his book Philip Yancey writes, "One detail in the Easter stories has always intrigued me. Why did Jesus keep the scars from his crucifixion? Presumably he could have had any resurrected body he wanted, and yet he chose one identifiable mainly by scars that could be seen and touched. Why?" Do you have any ideas?

3. Would you, like Thomas, have had to see Jesus to really believe he was risen—or would you have believed your friends and trusted that they were telling you the truth?

4. Think about your typical Easter celebration. What do you do on Easter? Does what you do reflect the importance of the Resurrection and the fact that this day defines your faith? Can you think of ways to make the celebration more significant?

Summary

In this session we:

- Discussed some of the ways we presently celebrate Easter.

- Examined what *really* happened on that first Easter.

- Focused on some of the doubts we have about Jesus' resurrection.

Suggested Reading

For more thoughts on this session's topic, read
"Resurrection: A Morning Beyond Belief,"
chapter 11 of *The Jesus I Never Knew*.

Session Twelve:
Ascension:
A Blank Blue Sky

Questions To Consider

- What was the ascension of Jesus and what impact has it had on the church?

- How are we fulfilling the "Great Commission?"

The Ascension

What was the ascension of Jesus?

Think of a time you had to say good-bye to someone you really cared about. How did you feel? What did you do? How do you think the disciples felt as they watched Jesus return to heaven?

How do you think you might have responded to this amazing event if you had been there?

Video Notes
Philip Yancey

Gospel Road

Jesus

Bible Study

Read Matthew 28:18–20

1. In his book Philip Yancey writes: "I have concluded that the Ascension represents my greatest struggle of faith—not whether it happened, but why. Would it not have been better if the Ascension had never happened? If Jesus had stayed on earth, he could answer our questions, solve our doubts, mediate our disputes of doctrine and policy. However, Jesus played his part and then left. Now it is up to us." What do you think?

2. What is the Great Commission? What does it mean to fulfill the Great Commission? As a church? As an individual? Do you think the Great Commission is realistic in our world?

Where is your World?

3. When are you most likely to compare God's call to you with his call to someone else? Do you ever shy away from service to God because you're intimidated by someone else or simply don't see a place for yourself? What do you need to do to begin to take Jesus' message seriously in your own life?

Summary

In this session we:

- Ascertained what the ascension of Jesus was and what kind of impact it had on the disciples and our world.

- Examined our lives in light of the Great Commission.

Suggested Reading

For more thoughts on this session's topic, read
"Ascension: A Blank Blue Sky,"
chapter 12 of *The Jesus I Never Knew*.

Session Thirteen:
Kingdom: Wheat Among the Weeds

Questions To Consider

- What *is* the kingdom?

- How can we best live out the kingdom and express Jesus' love?

Jesus' Second Coming

What comes to your mind when you think about the "end times"?

What meaning does Jesus' second coming have for you? Does it affect your life at all?

Video Notes
Philip Yancey

The Gospel According to St. Matthew

Son of Man

Bible Study

Read   Matthew 13:24–30, 36–43
        John 18:36–37
        Matthew 24:4–14

1. What is Jesus teaching us about his *kingdom* in these passages?

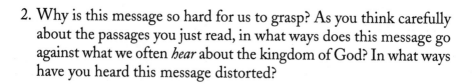

2. Why is this message so hard for us to grasp? As you think carefully
   about the passages you just read, in what ways does this message go
   against what we often *hear* about the kingdom of God? In what ways
   have you heard this message distorted?

Read John 17:20–23

1. How do you communicate Jesus' message of love?

2. What are some of the "evils of our society?" How can we confront these things and still communicate the love of Christ?

Summary

In this session we:

- Discussed the kingdom from the perspective of what we have learned from Philip Yancey and from our own understanding of the Scripture.

- Reflected upon how we can best live out the kingdom and express Jesus' love.

Suggested Reading

For more thoughts on this session's topic, read
"Kingdom: Wheat Among the Weeds,"
chapter 13 of *The Jesus I Never Knew*.

Session Fourteen:
The Difference He Makes

Questions To Consider

- How does Philip Yancey characterize Jesus?

- What difference has this course made on my understanding of Jesus?

Six Facets of Jesus' Life

Jesus is:

1. The sinless _____ of _____.

2. The _____-_____.

3. A portrait of _____.

4. The _____.

5. A portrait of _____.

6. The _____ _____.

Small Group Discussion

1. Refer to the six facets of Jesus' life listed on the previous page. Which do you most identify with?

2. One of the themes throughout this course has been Jesus' love. How does this square with your past understanding of Jesus? Have your views changed at all? Explain.

3. In his book Philip Yancey has written, "Jesus is radically unlike anyone else who has ever lived." Do you agree or disagree? Why did Jesus—his life and his message—have such a dramatic impact on *his* world? Why does it have an impact on *our* world?

Video Notes
Philip Yancey

This course has helped me to discover Jesus as . . .

Summary

In this session we:

• Learned about and discussed the different facets of Jesus' life.

• Shared our own discoveries of who Jesus is.

Suggested Reading

For more thoughts on this session's topic, read
"The Difference He Makes,"
chapter 14 of *The Jesus I Never Knew*.

About the Writer

Sheryl Moon is a consultant for various churches and organizations and a freelance writer. Her projects have ranged from designing a Christian education elective program for high school youth to writing guidebooks for video curriculum, including the *Saving Your Marriage Before It Starts* curriculum by Drs. Les and Leslie Parrott. Sheryl lives in Grand Rapids, Michigan, with her husband and son.

> "There is nothing we can do to make God love us more.
> There is nothing we can do to make God love us less."

We speak often of grace. But do we understand it? More important, do we truly *believe* in it . . . and do our lives proclaim it as powerfully as our words?

Grace is the church's great distinctive. It's the one thing the world cannot duplicate, and the one thing it craves above all else—for only grace can bring hope and transformation to a jaded world.

In this book, Yancey explores grace at street level. If grace is God's love for the undeserving, he asks, then what does it look like in action? And if Christians are its sole dispensers, then how are we doing at lavishing grace on a world that knows far more of cruelty and unforgiveness than it does of mercy?

Grace does not excuse sin, says Yancey, but it treasures the sinner. True grace is shocking, scandalous. It shakes our conventions with its insistence on getting close to sinners and touching them with mercy and hope.

In his most personal and provocative book ever, Yancey offers compelling, true portraits of grace's life-changing power. He searches for its presence in his own life and in the church. He asks, How can Christians contend graciously with moral issues that threaten all they hold dear?

And he challenges us to become living answers to a world that desperately wants to know, *What's So Amazing About Grace?*

Hardcover 0-310-21327-4
Audio Pages 0-310-21578-1
Study Guide 0-310-21904-3

Pick up your copy of *What's So Amazing About Grace?*
at Christian bookstores near you.

ZondervanPublishingHouse
Grand Rapids, Michigan 49530
http://www.zondervan.com

Look for these award-winning books by *Philip Yancey*

Where Is God When It Hurts?

A perennial best-seller, now in a revised and expanded edition, with a study guide. Yancey focuses on the role of pain in God's plan for life and how we can respond to it.

Softcover 0-310-35411-0
Mass Market 0-310-21437-8

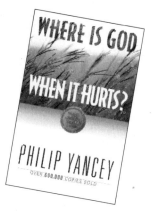

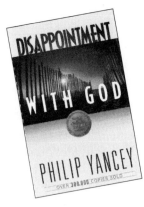

Disappointment with God

Philip Yancey answers the three questions no one asks aloud: Is God listening? Can he be trusted? And does he even exist? Yancey tackles the crisis of faith in this best-selling and award-winning book.

Softcover 0-310-51781-8

Church: Why Bother?

In this book about his own spiritual pilgrimage, Philip Yancey reflects on the church, his own perception of it, and the various metaphors the Bible uses to describe it. He challenges readers to find what's missing and to make their churches places of real community and spiritual vitality.

Hardcover 0-310-20200-0